T0157100

Fast Shopper, Slow Store

ALSO BY GARY SCHWARTZ

The Impulse Economy

Fast Shopper, Slow Store

A Guide to Courting and
Capturing the Mobile Consumer

Gary Schwartz

ATRIA PAPERBACK

New York   London   Toronto   Sydney   New Delhi

ATRIA PAPERBACK

A Division of Simon & Schuster, Inc.
1230 Avenue of the Americas
New York, NY 10020

First Atria Paperback edition September 2012

ATRIA PAPERBACK and colophon are trademarks of Simon & Schuster, Inc.

For information about special discounts for bulk purchases,
please contact Simon & Schuster Special Sales at 1-866-506-1949
or business@simonandschuster.com.

The Simon & Schuster Speakers Bureau can bring authors to
your live event. For more information or to book an event contact
the Simon & Schuster Speakers Bureau at 1-866-248-3049 or visit
our website at www.simonspeakers.com.

Designed by Nancy Singer

ISBN 978-1-4767-1870-5
ISBN 978-1-4767-0394-7 (ebook)

Contents

Intro to the Dating Guide

So the story goes: You walk into a bar, and there is a cute girl (guy) you'd like to hook up with. Even in this day and age, when both consenting adults probably have smartphones, you are unlikely to ask:

1. May I scan you?
2. Do you have a website address?
3. May I download your app?
4. Is there an NFC (Near Field Communication) tag somewhere on you that I can tap?

The natural question that you will ask is the same one your dad asked your mom (before the arrival of the smartphone):

5. May I have your number?

The phone was, and continues to be, a communication device. That elusive phone number in the bar is your way of connecting for a dinner date the next day. That magic number gives you the permission to call long after the bar is closed. It enables a two-way relationship. And it means, most important, that you are now in the other person's circle of trust.

The same holds true for retailers and brands; however, like a wide-eyed, socially awkward kid in the bar, in the digital era some retailers do not have the social tools to get the second date. They do not have the skills to build a trust relationship with anyone in the bar, and they are not in a position to get a simple phone number scrawled on the back of a proverbial matchbox.

In simpler times, you could put up a "store opening" sign and inflate a few dozen balloons, and consumers would file into your store. There was a time when a product could be sold based on a jingle, a flyer, a coupon.

You could neatly categorize your consumers and call them names such as "Traditional Tracey," "Stressed Susan," or "Variety-Loving Vicky." There seemed to be more order, and retailers' assumptions about shoppers always seemed to be accurate and measurable. The world was a safer place.

Those were the halcyon days when brands were at the center of the universe and shoppers orbited around them. Then something

An Instagram from the past*

---

* All photos taken via Instagram by my Samsung Note.

went awry. Retailers lost their mojo, and consumers began shopping around. Why go to the store when the store can come to me? they thought. Convenience trumped loyalty, and seemingly overnight many brands and retailers began orbiting alone.

It may feel as if digital technology has rudely disrupted the newspaper industry and music labels and is now reinventing the mall. However, it is not technology alone that is the culprit; retailers have not bothered to chase consumers and by not doing so have lost their connection to them. Bricks-and-mortar stores are not going away, but their business models and relationships to consumers are changing. The store's walls have become porous, and the science of plan-o-gramming,* shopper marketing, and customer loyalty has been thrown on its ear.

This book is about building the social tools necessary to reconnect with shoppers. For brands, retailers, and content owners that are trying to get out of a traditional relationship and back into the dating scene, this is a guide to how to connect with their new mobile consumers, get their phone numbers, and get that all-important second date.

---

* Diagram mapping the placement of retail products on shelves in order to maximize sales.

Elephants and Donkeys and Shampoo, Oh My!

SOAPBOX POLITICS • THIS SEAT'S TAKEN • MORE THAN KISSING BABIES

Many people in the business of connecting to retail customers are busy reworking their game plan. It may reassure the reader that no one is immune to digital disruption, which has left most industry folk, from brands to broadcasters, from publishers to politicians, questioning the way they engage with their audiences.

The 2012 U.S. presidential election is a perfect example of brands desperately seeking buyers. As the candidates claw for positioning, it is evident that the election process is (surprisingly or not) similar to selling a product in a hugely competitive retail market. Each electoral cycle demonstrates the challenge of courting an increasingly digital public.

The techniques that President Barack Obama and Mitt Romney use to market their platform and gather votes are the same as those embraced by brands to manage their market presence, build engagement, and move their audience to a sale. All the challenges of chasing the itinerant mobile public are the same as those facing bewildered shopkeepers.

Soapbox Politics

Products are bought based on their function or the service that they deliver, brand recall, brand loyalty, convenience, and, of course, price. The same holds true for the presidential race. The candidates all have something to sell:

- A *product*
- A *service*
- A *price*

The *product* they are marketing is themselves. Republican candidate Mitt Romney's campaign managers, for instance, are trying to sell Romney the man, the father, the ex-governor, the future president, and the businessman. They do this in a number of ways: by optimizing his camera appeal, wardrobe, personality, and ability to look good in a fifteen-second media sound bite.

The *service* they are offering is outlined in their platform: their policies, their ideas, and their vision. A campaign, like a retail store, is selling a product with an appealing exterior and the promise of a rewarding interior.

The *price* is the cost of implementing the service. There is a fine political dance of costs and benefits as politicians attempt to keep various—and often opposing—factions happy.

A candidate stands on a podium; a product sits on a shelf. Their quandary is the same.

In the case of retail there is a science to closing the sale. What shopkeepers and brands call the "path to purchase" explores the shopper's experience—from the first time we hear a product jingle to the moment we bring the product home—and can involve everything from the $75 billion that is still spent annually on television advertising to recipes on YouTube videos to dog-eared coupons.

This is the step-by-step process of moving possible customers to purchase (wherever that purchase may happen).

What are Romney and Obama's biggest concerns? Of the American public that historically engages in the political debate, many do *not* end up voting. According to Pew Research Center data (http://people-press.org/files/legacy-questionnaires/295.pdf), a week before the 2006 midterm elections, 68 percent of would-be voters said they were registered and planned to vote in the upcoming election; however, on election day only 40 percent of eligible adults actually voted. Any candidate who wants to live in the White House needs to answer this marketing and sales dilemma: why did motivated and engaged citizens not cast a ballot? 2000 was the only year over the past two decades when expressed engagement mirrored actual turnout in the presidential election.

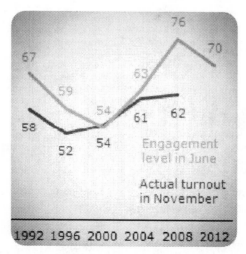

Path to purchase (interrupted?)
Pew Research Center data, June 7–17, 2012
(turnout figures based on voting-eligible population)

Closing a sale is key; it is all that really matters. A campaign team knows that whether it is packaging Romney or a household staple, all is for naught if it cannot move someone into the voting booth (or, in the case of a store, to a cash register). We need to convince the voter/shopper to select one product/candidate over another. We need him or her to make this decision at the ballot box—what brands call the "moment of truth."

The biggest challenge for a brand trying to court and capture the mobile public is that buyers are no longer captive in stores. This is hugely inconvenient. If shoppers are not orbiting the storefront, where do you find them? If you do not know what path they are on, how can you post effective signs?

Whether in the ballot box or in a store, our attention spans are becoming increasingly deficient. At home, consumers may write out shopping lists and do hours of product research, but in a store, the majority of their basket is made up of products bought on impulse. Billions of dollars are spent to try to influence this public. To create an affinity for a candidate or a shampoo, how can we best encourage mobile consumers to buy our product over another one?

This Seat's Taken

The path to the White House is challenging. The public is consuming information, signs, and messages on smaller screens—screens that we no longer control or even influence effectively. Digital natives (those born into a nonlinear world, unlike many of us analogue immigrants) are at ease navigating a handheld screen on which there is limited space for traditional signs. Adding complexity, digital natives move through nearly thirty windows on that screen per hour.

What we say, how we say it, and where and by whom are all key factors in our success or failure to connect with mobile consumers. During the midterm election, the Pew Research Center's *The Internet and Campaign 2010* report found that 42 percent of survey respondents said that political information they saw or read online had encouraged them to vote for or against a specific candidate. It may seem encouraging that www.whitehouse.gov mobile traffic has grown from 3 percent to nearly 8 percent over the last year; however, so has traffic to information sites beyond the control of the old guard's information peddlers.

Gone are the days when candidates could rely exclusively on broadcast media sound bites. Hot-or-not media culture is still a factor in winning the race; however, we have moved from a 1.0 to a 2.0 campaign, where the winner needs to do more than shout out slogans from the caboose of a train or playing the saxophone on late-night television.

Are we building relationships or just posting traffic signs?

Digital appears to offer a new platform. Obama had 45,000 Twitter followers four years ago; now he has approximately 20 million. However, though this is undoubtedly a powerful distribution channel, most of the dialogue is happening *between* voters. What role does the candidate play in interpersonal channels? Most voters' digital conversations take place on social networks that are not directly tied to the candidates' soapboxes. Though Twitter channels can nudge images and text to followers; beyond this limited broadcast function, the ensuing conversation is out of their control. Ten percent of the public use mobile devices to dialogue with one another during election debates, and 14 percent have told others they voted (http://pewinternet.org/Reports/2010/Mobile-Politics.aspx).

Historically, when we couldn't control conversations, we invested in messaging platforms and messaging rails. The London Olympics' Walk A Mile social engagement campaign is a good

The State Department gets it!

example.* The State Department, along with the President's Challenge, is supporting a fitness and global engagement engine to reach its target audience.

We have become an "authenticity" culture, and it is difficult (if not impossible) to manufacture community. Everything we consume has to be validated by the blogosphere, Facebook, Twitter, Pinterest, and other peer-to-peer media channels. Even the *New York Times* journalist and self-professed Luddite David Carr acknowledges that "the messages are the media now."

Elections can no longer be won by selling the candidates in the traditional way. But how are the candidates working outside the retail store model and moving voters into a trusted long-term relationship that will influence their decision at the voting booth?

We are the measure not of our tweets (messages) but rather of our retweets—that is, messages that demonstrate social affirmation and loyalty.

More Than Kissing Babies

So what builds a credible relationship with our audience? In 2012, this is what gets a president and a brand selected. These are the social CliffsNotes for any aspiring brand:

- **Think messaging.** According to the Pew Research Center, 68 percent of smartphone owners open fewer than six apps per week. (Only .25 percent of voters used a political mobile app during the midterm election.) Do not get caught focusing on building comprehensive websites or applications. Focus on simple, personal channels.

---

* www.2012walkamile.com

- **Think targeting.** Attention-challenged small-screen-using consumers need relevant, targeted communication. Know your audience. And, more important, make sure your audience feels you know them. (Rick Santorum was a poster child for this. He enabled each of his state teams to customize local messaging.)

- **Think authenticity.** Move from politics 1.0 to 2.0 and join the conversation. (Obama's NCAA basketball bracket challenge to voters will go further than Obama adopting a mobile photo app or Instagram. The former shows authenticity; the latter seems like trying too hard.)

- **Think screen.** Screens have become the windows to our audience. The television in every living room is now the tablet in the bedroom and the handheld on the train. Each screen demands different messaging.

- **Think narrative.** Voters are channel-indifferent. Move with them through the Web, various mobile devices, and live media appearances. Create a consistent message and a consistent engagement strategy.

- **Think frictionless.** Count clicks to voter conversion. Our attention is constantly being pulled in different directions—we can't be sold with layers of complex media, and we are averse to wasting our time filling out forms. Make all messages, surveys, and feedback opportunities actionable with a single click.

The key for politicians is to focus on mobile messaging, mobile engagement, mobile trust, and building a long-term relationship. For the brand this means it needs to get off the shelf and perhaps even leave the mall.

Barnes & Noble:
Store, Library, Museum

SMELL THE PAGES! THE BOOKSTORE
AS THE CANARY OF THE MALL

The bookstore was modeled on the library—a quiet, sacred place where lovers of books went to commune. It is still is. But bookstore owners forgot that libraries were intended to browse in and not to sell product. The bookstore has become entertainment: we smell the book pages, we sit and drink coffee. However, we end up buying tchotchkes for our living room rather than books.

Many publishers have started shipping books directly to stores, since bookstores' warehouses have become chaotic depots for chairs, lamps, and pillows. It may be too late for bookstores to reaffirm their value proposition and find a way of reintroducing their mission-critical role into the digital mall. The entire retail value chain is changing.

The bookstore, like its hapless counterparts, the video store and electronics store, has hit hard times. The industry is second-guessing itself:

- Could a smarter Kodak have built Instagram?

- Could a smarter Blockbuster have launched Netflix?
- Can a nondigital business disrupt and grow new business methodology from within?

As shopping goes digital, stores need to find ways to bridge physical and virtual shopping carts. How can a terrestrial store strike a balance between its role in the mall and its role in the Internet cloud?

Barnes & Noble executives are undoubtedly aware (as Borders executives before them) that the 2010s are eerily reminiscent of the music industry in the 2000s. Books, reading, and commerce behavior has changed. The relationship between shopper and store has changed.

The bookstore may be a contrived notion. A mobile device enables goods and services to be sold in context. A yoga studio, doctor's office, or movie theater is perhaps a more context-rich storefront for books than a bookstore. The book should not be the focus; spirituality, health, or a movie should be at the top of consumers' minds, and the physical book or its digital version should be readily available to be searched, scanned, tapped, or texted on demand.

Smell the Pages!

Does this mean good riddance to bookstores, publishers, agents? Perhaps there is a new, more efficient order in town? Perhaps a new, streamlined business model would be both good for consumers and good for the industry long term?

The book industry has not changed much over the years. Writers email their pitch letters to agents. Agents establish trusted relationships with publishers. The process is not easy. J. K. Rowling's agent submitted her wizard's tale to twelve publishing houses and was rejected twelve times before she finally found a home. She is in good company: Stephen King and George Orwell were also rejected. One of Orwell's critics wrote on the back of the *Animal Farm* manuscript, "It is impossible to sell animal stories in the USA."

As the blog "Literary Rejections on Display" notes, "Remember this: Someone out there will always say no." With Amazon.com's self-publishing business, that is no longer the case. Amazon.com always says yes.

There are inspirational tales of authors such as Karen McQuestion, who, after giving up on publishing her book *A Scattered Life*, managed to self-publish and sell more than 35,000 copies. Jim Kukral, the author of *This Book Will Make You Money*, says, "The walls are crumbling down, and aggressive and smart entrepreneurs are running through the gates to grab their share of self-publishing gold."

But is the new bookstore in the cloud sustainable? There are questions.

The number of self-published titles in the United States has tripled over the past few years and will continue to grow. However, by cutting out the agency and publisher value chain, the industry has made the online and mobile storefront into the Wild West. Publishing has become the easy part. Selling and driving profit for authors has become difficult. Similar to the flood of self-published apps on the iPhone storefront, there is a point where it is difficult for a title to be found.

We all know that what Amazon.com calls "pro-consumer" has been a major business disruptor for bookstores and now shoe, apparel, and electronics stores. Could Amazon.com simply using books to build its m-commerce empire? Is the book industry a necessary sacrifice: mobile commerce road kill?

The Bookstore as the Canary of the Mall

Here are some historical bullet points on how the bookstore was turned on its ear. Maybe there is some guidance here for the remaining mall tenants?

1. **Bad-Boy Barnes & Noble:** In the 1990s, Barnes & Noble opened superstore after superstore across the United States. It become the Walmart of books, with the same attitude toward vendors. Publishers were forced to grin and bear the harsh Barnes & Noble business terms: challenging discounts, slingshot mechanized return policies, and more. Smaller publishers and independent bookstores began to vanish.

2. **The rise of the e-book:** In 2007, we saw the first Kindle, the harbinger of a new power game and, more important, a new relationship with the mobile consumer. The Kindle became the new storefront, further threatening the first market disrupter, Barnes & Noble. In order to promote the Kindle, Amazon.com sold electronic books below wholesale price. It took a loss for a tactical reason: owning the commerce platform was its ultimate goal.

3. **Counterattack:** This revenue model is understandably suboptimal for publishers. Led by the New York–based Macmillan, the industry challenged Amazon.com's hostile business model. Amazon.com pulled Macmillan content from its site. Macmillan held ground. Amazon.com caved.

4. **Slippery slope:** Bookstores (e.g., Barnes & Noble) and publishers (e.g., Simon & Schuster, Penguin, Hachette) launched self-publishing e-book services (PubIt! and Bookish, respectively).

With all the stakeholders playing all the roles, the value chain is breaking up.

5. **The Kindle Fire:** Combining commerce with the immersive Kindle experience is the final frontier. Allowing the armchair reader to purchase with ease is a natural and powerful evolution of the bookstore. Amazon.com is so confident about this that it is selling the unit at a loss ($199 for a unit that costs $210 to make).

6. **Kindle Owners' Lending Library:** Amazon Prime members who own a Kindle can "borrow" one title per month for free from Amazon.com's expanding library. Presently, there are a limited number of books available; Amazon.com did not receive consent to include titles from many publishers. In some cases, it simply pays the wholesale price for the book each time somebody borrows it. Is this the new Napster, the original peer-to-peer music file-sharing service, but legal and underwritten by Amazon.com?

7. **Amazon.com as store:** Is the online retailer finally closing the loop by opening a physical showroom? Rumors abound that Amazon.com will pilot a store in its hometown of Seattle to showcase the Kindle Fire tablet. Is this a stepping-stone to an Apple-like Genius Bar for books?

This seems to be the seven-bullet epitaph for the bookstore. John Biggs blogs nostalgically, "While I will miss the creak of the Village Bookshop's old church floor, the calm of Crescent City books, and the crankiness of the Provincetown Bookshop, the time has come to move on."

Move on? The question is, where to?

Best Buy: Cloud Meets Mall

HOW CYBER MONDAY BECAME CYBER FRIDAY •
THE SEVEN-INCH MALL BUSTER • DARK CLOUDS

The mall is evolving or devolving, depending on what role you play in the value chain. There are clear winners and losers. Best Buy has become one of the mall losers.

In 1983, the company opened its first superstore in Roseville, Minnesota, offering a wide product selection and discounts on brand-name products that drew shoppers away from more expensive smaller electronics stores. Best Buy was a retail innovator, cornering the electronics market across the United States and expanding globally. But somewhere this big-box retail giant lost its way.

Maybe Best Buy's decline dates back to 2009, when Circuit City exited the mall. And then more measurably to 2010, when shoppers stopped hunting down the Best Buy sales representatives, the all-knowing "blue shirts," and started using their phones as a product research resource. As phones became more powerful, the busy blue shirts seemed less essential, almost dispensable. Clerks had less access to technology than the sophisticated, swaggering smartphone-toting shoppers.

Best Buy, like many successful companies, has become disintermediated by technology. I disagree with retail critics who say that Best Buy was asleep at the wheel. That is far too trite an analysis. The company undoubtedly saw the writing on the wall years ago. The problem was that the writing said, "You're in trouble!" It (unfortunately) didn't say exactly what the megacompany should do about it.

So what led to Best Buy's decline? You can criticize Best Buy's customer service issues. You can point to the pop philosophy of Tony Hsieh at Amazon.com's online shoe and apparel company, Zappos, who grew his business by making returns simple, not taxed by restocking fees and other hidden surprises. However, the fundamental issue is that Best Buy could not seamlessly connect its Internet cloud to its store experience.

I recall a discussion between Target's and Best Buy's digital leads in San Francisco three years ago at a retail leadership event. The iPad had just arrived in stores, and they talked excitedly about how the mobile shop could help customers navigate the store. No one, however, acknowledged the danger of their customers navigating their store through a competitor's cloud.

Like with many retail leviathans, a price-conscious shopper will find significant price disparity between the store's online and in-store products. Best Buy may valiantly offer a "lower price guarantee" for competitive products in-store, in print or online; however, its online store cautions: "Online prices and selection generally match our retail stores, but may vary." In many cases this may vary significantly. Perhaps its biggest competitor is its own siloed business units.

Best Buy's robust digital storefront and its innovative "grab-and-go" express self-service storefronts in airports could not save its ailing big boxes. A month before Best Buy missed its revenue targets in spring 2012, laying off four hundred employees and announcing the closing of fifty big-box stores, it sent out a memo:

This closure is consistent with Best Buy's stated goal of reducing overall square footage by 10-percent in the next three to five years while also increasing our points of presence in different ways.

Best Buy needed a "different way." It had lost touch with the shoppers. It stopped dating; the love it used to feel from its consumers is gone.

How Cyber Monday Became Cyber Friday

Back on November 28, 2005, Shop.org, a trade association for online retailers, started discussing an online shopping phenomenon following Thanksgiving shopping that it called "Cyber Monday." After fighting for deals in the aisles, shoppers starting surfing the Web for remnant deals.

This online shopping cloud (which was situated on a separate day, with separate deals for online shoppers) is now moving into our prime-time shopping calendar. Most mobile shopping on Black Friday still tends to be mobile marketing–focused: price comparison hunting with Amazon.com's Price Check, ShopSavvy, or eBay's RedLaser app; mobile coupon clipping for show-to-save deals that drive impulse shopper traffic or what retailers call "door swing" into the mall and retail store.

Over the 2011 holiday season, Amazon.com launched a "pro-consumer" promotion that offered shoppers 5 percent off cloud purchases if they price-checked using Amazon.com's mobile app while in a physical store.

Retailers were in a furor. However, that was just the beginning, Amazon.com's opening salvo. Mobile phone helped shoppers better navigate high-value items such as shoes and electronics in their local mall. While the price-check services were used by hard-core bargain hunters to keep stores honest, it is still early days. The small-screen experience was *not* optimal for actually purchasing on a phone.

Nevertheless, the mobile phone was certainly starting to inter-rupt in-aisle purchases. If Price Check showed a better deal online, many folks closed their phone and chose to buy the item that evening on the Web on a large screen in the comfort of their home.

When the Apple iPad arrived, many thought that it would move commerce into the street. In fact, though you see intrepid street warriors navigating with their iPads, the device was designed primarily as an in-home device. Though I have seen tablets used on escalators (and even balanced on urinals) their main goal is to help folks browse the Internet anywhere from the kitchen to the couch.

The iPad is a revolution because it seamlessly and elegantly hy-bridizes:

- Mobile and fixed Internet
- Small screen and large screen

Other tablets have entered the market on Apple's terms and have had mixed results; however, that is about to change. The tablet is getting off the couch and moving into the mall.

The Seven-Inch Mall Buster

At-home purchases are moving into the store aisle. There is a new breed of shopping disruption entering the market. And it is the seven-inch tablet.

The Kindle Fire and Google Nexus tablet are all about one-click commerce. While these devices provide a rich entertainment interface, they are also optimized for in-store, in-mall deal hunting, price comparison, and, most important, one-click checkout. The new commerce tablet is a portable mall buster.

These palm-held tablets may be the final commerce frontier. Amazon.com and Google are so confident about the commerce that they will generate in the mall that they are selling the units at a door-buster price of $199. The seven-inch black slab fits (extremely snugly) in your jacket pocket or purse, ready to interrupt the shopper's path to purchase.

The first Kindle Fire is Wi-Fi-bound, but rumors are that there is a 4G version of Kindle Fire as well as a Kindle Phone in the cards. (Will it have a scanner built in to help shoppers check inventory in the Internet cloud?)

Amazon.com's and Google's one-click commerce, along with Visa's V.me service, Buck's Single Click Checkout, iTunes' EasyPay, LightningBuy, and a flood of other cloud commerce options are entering the market.

What does this mean? It means that on Friday, November 23, 2012, and Friday, November 22, 2013, shoppers will move from comparison price hunting in the mall to *disruptive purchasing in the cloud.* No longer are Cyber Monday and Black Friday neatly separated: the cloud is in the mall to stay.

Dark Clouds

RetailTraffic, an industry publication, anticipated more than five thousand store closings in North America in 2012—up nearly 40 percent from 2011. Many will be due to continuing shopper malaise, but as in-mall cloud shopping accelerates, many stores in the apparel and electronics vertical sectors will need to reinvent themselves. Retailers need to focus on breaking down the channel barriers between their physical stores and their online presence. Tackling "cross-channel disconnect" will be the key to survival.

Stores will need to focus on the non–Black Friday days—all 364 of them—and work to build a loyal, one-to-one relationship with shoppers, using their phones to connect their store experience with their cloud experience.

Content curation, sensory experience, customer service, and love are all a store has. It will not win on price alone.

Amazon.com:
Store as Showroom

SHOWROOMING • THE NEED TO CLIENTELE •
THE STORE OF THE FUTURE

Shoppers are impulse consumers. They buy in the aisle, in what retailers call "five by five" (five seconds by five feet). At home they may write out lengthy shopping lists and do hours of research on products, but in a store 80 percent of their basket is made up of products bought on *impulse.*

The phone has become a shopping aid that can help shoppers be more effective impulse buyers. This is the industry's challenge: the retailers that manage to engage effectively with these new shoppers will win.

I have always said that the phone in a shopper's pocket is more powerful than the computer that sent the first person to the moon. Recently I was doing some water-cooler math with my IT director. We worked out that the Apollo Guidance Computer (ACG) had 2 kilobytes of memory, 32 kilobytes of read-only memory (storage), and a CPU running at 1.024 megahertz; the new Samsung Galaxy S III has 64 gigabytes of memory, 64 gigabytes of storage, and a quad-core CPU running at 1.4 gigahertz.

Slow phone booth, fast phone

That means the hand-sized shopping aid is essentially *2,600 times* as fast as the computer that sent the rocket to the moon. But that's just raw speed. It is clear that stores that do not know how to engage effectively on this superphone are under siege.

Showrooming

We know that shoppers like to try before they buy. We need to touch and fondle products before making the decision to take them home. However in a world where touch, trial, and purchase do not necessarily take place in the same store, many retailers are in a quandary.

The technical term for this retail malady is "showrooming," the phenomenon of going to a store to look at and touch a product and then checking it out in the cloud (unfortunately, in many cases, a competitor's cloud).

We know that Blockbuster, Borders, and Circuit City have all fallen to the efficiencies of the Internet. We know that Barnes & Noble, Target, and Best Buy are going through bumpy times.

Retailers are flummoxed about how to respond. Many have tried to leverage the phone and the new digital channel, but many still consider the phone a threat, not an opportunity.

Target went to the length of sending a letter to its suppliers that read, "What we aren't willing to do is let online-only retailers use our brick-and-mortar stores as a showroom for their products and undercut our prices without making investments, as we do, to proudly display your brands." Signed sincerely and remorsefully, Gregg Steinhafel, the CEO of Target.

Amazon.com clearly feels that its success with the Price Check app is a good indicator that the new Kindle Fire tablet will be the mobile commerce device of choice. Amazon.com sees its role as "pro-consumer," and if what consumers care about is price, it is right.

If the retail industry continues to lament the rise of "show-rooming," is it simply crying "Uncle" to Amazon.com? For Target to place unique products in store that cannot be price-checked on Amazon.com is not a sustainable answer. Turning off Wi-Fi or making the product tag difficult to scan will not work.

Many retailers do not acknowledge that the internet, if used correctly, can be a boon to their in-store business. Much of Google's advertising pitch is based on what it refers to as the science of O2S (online to store) or ROPO (research online, purchase offline). The shopper moves from the store into the cloud but also moves, as fluidly, from the cloud into the store.

The top three factors in shopper decision making are *price, convenience,* and *trust.* If shopping is all about price, we should all close up store and go home. Convenience can work for the cloud and bricks and mortar. Trust is the silver bullet.

A shopkeeper needs to use the mobile channel to develop a digital relationship with loyal shoppers. Until about twenty-four months ago a shopper needed a clerk to navigate a store. A shopper needed a clerk to find information on a product. Remember lining up to speak to a person in a blue shirt in a Best Buy store? As discussed previously, the blue shirts now have inferior technology and less access to information than a shopper with a handheld device.

The Need to Clientele

If you walk into the new C. Wonder store at 72 Spring Street in New York City, you will notice that there are no cash registers. This is a store designed by digital natives who did not have to contend with the old point-of-sale terminals of the bygone age. C. Wonder sales representatives walk the floor and can cash shoppers out in aisles using a mobile point-of-sale device. This enables a seamless and personable try-and-buy experience. Digital natives demand digital clienteling.

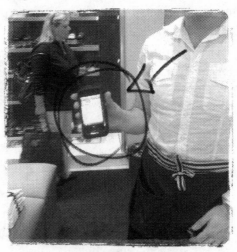

A mobile checkout in C. Wonder

"Clienteling" is a retail term that predates "mobile"; it is the act of interacting with shoppers to provide personalized service, offers, and communication in a store. The modern version of clienteling is mobile by design, neatly packaged on a tablet, held in the shop assistant's arm.

Retailers need to use tablets and handhelds to interact with shoppers; help them find products; add something to a wish list and tie the wish list to a profile; ask the shopper for her email address or phone number to send updates, sale reminders, and VIP invites. Retailers need to engage shoppers at the cash register and all other retail touch points to capture consumers' contact information for follow-on deals and offers and general relationship building.

Cross-channel disconnect is where most retail revenue is lost: between the store and the online site. Clienteling enables shop-keepers to connect bricks-and-mortar shoppers with their online experience and develop a trust relationship that will keep them as loyal customers.

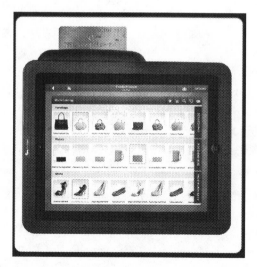

Curating your digital wish list in bricks and mortar

The Store of the Future

GameStop is demonstrating that showrooming is a viable business. It has redesigned its stores as portals to the Web. It has combined online games with packaged goods. Its store of the future is full of connected devices with downloadable games and demos. Game-Stop is focused on two things: How can it move its half-billion physical storegoers into its cloud to buy digital game content? How can it better curate gamers' online shopping experience in store?

But GameStop not only changed its retail plan-o-gram (store layout), it also changed its business model. It bought Jolt Online Gaming, a maker of free-to-play online games. It also bought Kongregate, an indie online game portal. Together they have made both its store *and* its product offering cross-channel.

Stores such as GameStop that manage to develop a digital trust relationship across all their retail touch points will encourage impulse shoppers to make impulse buys at their checkouts (wherever they may be).

Sony was an early mover in the showroom space, opening a dozen Sony-style stores to demonstrate its products. Unfortunately, the model is not always easy to crack. Sony downsized to one supershowroom in Century City, Los Angeles, designed by the retail wondersmith Klein Dytham, who designed Tokyo's Sephora flagship store and Selfridges' "The Wonder Room" luxury emporium in London. However impressive this Century City store may be, Sony needs to find a way to extend this store experience to every mall in North America. A tremendously costly undertaking. Samsung has also moved hesitantly into retail, opening new brand stores globally from Toronto, Canada, to Nairobi, Kenya. These are not committed showroom strategies.

Apple is the only manufacturer that has succeeded in moving from brand showroom to commercial success. The Apple Store defined the concept of creating a play space for Apple's aspirational shoppers. Apple's blue shirts are a new generation of sales clerks; they use their own product to sell their product. They build trust—*I am an Apple fanboy too*—and focus on relationship building in the store.

Should Samsung, LG, Toshiba, and other Best Buy squatters aggressively open their own showrooms in malls, or can a new breed of retail aggregator play the trusted sales clerk role by using smart clienteling in stores to connect stores with *their* cloud checkout?

Will this showroom be Amazon or a reinvented Best Buy? It may not be an incumbent at all. Somewhere between Best Buy downsizing and Amazon.com learning how to sell in bricks and mortar, we will likely see a new model arise.

Tesco: The Paper Store

SCREENAGERS • TRAIN STATIONS AND THE NEW SCREENS • REINVENTING PAPER • DWELL TIME

This is a picture of my eighteen-year-old daughter doing her homework. As in most households, the reader may agree, she resembles the average young adult raised on a healthy digital diet.

Digital native in the wild

- Large screen: Four windows open: Tumblr, Gmail, TV, Google Docs
- Medium screen: Facebook
- Small screen: SMS, Instagram

Time Inc. observed twenty-year-olds and found that people who had grown up on digital media surf through twenty-seven screens per hour. These native digital folk multitasked 35 percent more than their nonnative digital brethren. My colleague Chetan Sharma's research shows that the average number of connected screens in a US household is five, with over 6 percent of homes having more than fifteen connected devices.

It is not only screens that are important but where those screens are active. Seventy-five percent are active on phones in the john, with 13 percent of guys completing mobile purchases there (www.11mark.com/IT-in-the-Toilet).

Toilet-based commerce

Screenagers

Screens and media consumption have changed. To understand how to sell, we have to start by understanding the complex matrix of screens and realize that our self-constructed divisions between the store and the checkout are slowly disappearing. There is no longer a dividing line between bricks and mortar, billboards, and screens on our phones.

Now, with Google Goggles, a consumer can surf the Internet, locate stores, shop, snap photos, start video chats, and serenade his girlfriend, all through a pair of stylish G+ lenses (www.youtube. com/watch?v=9c6W4CCU9M4).

We are left with only two states: *screens* (media) and *actions* (consumption).

Actions change depending on the screen. Each screen has a personality and lifestyle. Microsoft looked at screen "personalities" globally and tried to classify the various relationships that consumers have with each screen. It created the following nomenclature for the four major screen types:

- Television is the *entertainer.*
- PC is the *sage.*
- Tablet is the *wizard.*
- Handheld is the *lover:* the last screen consumers look at before they fall asleep and the first one they reach for when they get up.

Each screen is separate but contiguous. This multiscreen economy has become pivotal to the success of the industry. The chairman of Nokia uses the screen as a key reason why Windows will become more relevant in 2013 with its new Surface tablet:

> For the first time in the history of technology, the Windows
> Phone 8 operating system makes it possible for users to
> have the same experience on a PC, tablet or smartphone,
> and for many people on their televisions via their gaming
> consoles, and to do the same thing almost seamlessly from
> one screen to the next.

All screen software developers are standardizing their device experience. Android's Ice Cream Sandwich and Jelly Bean operating system were developed to be cross-platform and function seamlessly across tablets and handhelds.

However, though the screens are contiguous, each is used for different actions and requires a different media treatment. I start bidding on an item on eBay on a midsize-screen tablet; however, I continue the bidding on a small screen in the few seconds dwell time at a red light or while waiting for an elevator. I research and buy a product at home on a thoughtful large screen; however, I compare prices in a store on a screen that fits into my pocket.

Though information and commerce need to flow seamlessly across all screens, each one has its own DNA and plays a unique role in consumers' lives:

> Digital billboard → TV → Game console → Laptop → iPad
> tablet → 7-inch Kindle Fire → Samsung Note → Hand-
> held → In-store payment terminal screen

Ergonomically, screens can be divided into three types:

1. Digital billboards, TVs, and Laptops are *freestanding* (on a lap or other support).
2. Tablets are *two-fisted* (they are portable but immobilize the consumer).

Verizon's mobile mandala

3. Note and handheld are *one-fisted* (they enable in-store multi-
   tasking).

The ergonomics of the device (how we hold it, how we navigate) influence the actions we take and in turn dictate the content
that retailers and brands need to create for each type of screen. The
one-fisted device is the most interesting to me, as it plays the role
of the mouse, the click. It enables all other screens, locations, and
products to be actionable.

Brands have taken to redesign this digital narrative using the
small mobile screen as the lowest common denominator. Li-Ning,
a sportswear company with no physical storefront in the United
States, started with a handset version of its store and then expanded
it to larger-format screens, forcing retailers to think simple. (It is
an old technique and something digital designers need to note. The
playwright Samuel Beckett wrote his plays in his second language,
French, and then translated them into his native English to force

himself to keep brevity and focus. Likewise, brands need to design their screens from small to big, from limited to expansive.)

Train Stations and the New Screens

In 1888, the Thomas Adams Gum Company's revolutionary candy dispenser appeared on New York City train platforms. Adams' Tutti-Frutti gum dispensers, although primitive, were pure genius, capitalizing on the dwell time of the consumer on the platform. Those self-service storefronts became an instant success.

Candy sellers could now sell twenty-four hours a day with minimum overhead. With a few modifications, cigarettes, beverages, condoms, and even hot meals began dropping out of dispensing machines.

The message was clearly advertised on the first candy dispenser: SAVE TIME. The promise was instant access to product anywhere, anytime.

Train stations are disruptive places. More than a hundred years

1900 New York City Transit platform

Appealing to the 1900 mobile commuter

later, in train stations in Seoul, Berlin, and New York City a new kind of futuristic grocery and cosmetic dispenser appeared, possibly heralding a more significant convenience revolution for the shopper. The store is made of paper, the machine is the consumer's phone, and the product is dispensed via the Internet.

PayPal's Singapore subway paper storefront, Valentine's Day 2012

I listened to a keynote address by a PayPal representative on February 14, 2012, as the company unveiled its new last-minute Valentine's Day shopping in fifteen subway stations in Singapore. Many people have seen a picture of Tesco's South Korea mobile supermarket: a Korean commuter with phone raised shopping for milk and vegetables as he waits for a subway train to pull into the station.

PayPal and Tesco are converting advertising space into a point of sale. Product images are simply printed on panels with accompanying 2D scannable codes, and the purchased goods are delivered to the consumer's home. All that this new kind of store requires is a media buy: the advertising panels on a subway, mall, or bus shelter. By moving the store onto plastic and paper, the store transfers much of the cost of store operations to consumers and their phones.

Reinventing Paper

A phone can make a paper display interactive. More important, it makes it interactive with a personal device that enables retailers and brands to transact commerce and establish an opt-in to communicate outside the store. Shoppers bring $500-plus smartphones into the mall, and retailers and brands that do not reinvent their media and business models to interface with those devices are missing the new storefront.

Many Stateside who saw the photos of South Koreans shopping using their phones in front of pictures in a subway station asked: "Is this the new store?" Is this retail 3.0?

Everyone seems excited, vying to be the first to launch versions of a paper storefront:

- The pharmacy franchise Budnikowsky was the first to sell products off a paper poster in train stations in Berlin.

- *Glamour* magazine was the first to sell cosmetics via mobile phones off backlit billboards in New York.
- Simon & Schuster was the first publisher to use Near Field Communication tabs on their books to allow readers to tap their phone to receive digital content in Los Angeles.

In all of the above examples the phone is the kiosk, the wallet, and the content dispenser, all at the same time. The idea is very appealing, and the public relations spin is worth the effort. It is certainly a sign of disruption but not the death knell of the store. In truth, Tesco used it as a publicity stunt in a country where it does not have the bricks-and-mortar advantage of the two already existing convenience store chains. I would hazard a guess that the traffic generated by Tesco in South Korea, Budnikowsky's poster in Germany, and the *Glamour* storefront in the United States was modest. However, all of those pilots succeeded in making the consumer look, and that is, most probably, considered a successful outcome.

Dwell Time

A virtual storefront based on plastic and paper may not seem like a substantial retail innovation; however, in many ways it could ultimately be as profound as the first vending machine that appeared in the United States a hundred years ago. This new paper store, powered by a tap or scan of a consumer's phone, can play a new role somewhere between the physical store and the online storefront.

Ultimately this new store can become a creative advertising unit that will allow any media to become a commerce driver: a *mobile commerce advertising unit.* We can now layer in purchase anywhere. This is as relevant to a subway as it is to a magazine. Now, for the first time:

Product + Purchase intent = Sale

There is no path to purchase. With cosmetics, electronics, apparel, books, and a host of other products, we are already on the consumer's doorstep. Unless we are selling grocery store–bound baked beans or bananas, we no longer need to map a circuitous route from "That looks nice" to "Where can I buy it?"

A store can be embedded into a cosmetics feature in a magazine. It can be a small bookstore in a cinema selling books related to the film or in a Babies "R" Us selling "So this is your first baby" books. Products can be more strategic and contextual and stimulate more purchases.

Let's look at Best Buy's Express's "grab-and-go" vending machines in airports. Perfect for "I need to grab the product there and now." However, if I want to send a product to a friend or ship it to my destination, Best Buy could simply buy the airport media displays on the left and right of the unit and title one "Gift-and-Go" and the other "Ship-and-Go." For the small cost of a media buy it has tripled its "storefront."

Grab a phone and go mobile

The paper store is ideal for any "dwell" places where people hang out and look at the walls for entertainment:

- Public transportation
- Transit shelters
- Airport battery-charging stations
- Starbucks

Better yet, targeted products can be sold in dwell locations that are *context-rich:*

- Doctors' waiting rooms (health-related products)
- Movie theaters (books on which movies are based)
- Yoga spas (spirituality and wellness products)
- Agency lobbies ("Fast shopper. Slow store" :))

We now can hybridize digital and physical commerce. A virtual dispenser does not require inventory checks, power, or refrigeration to work. The consumer is the one who has bought the $500 smartphone, giving her the power to activate the plastic and paper call to action.

This is a new retail space that leverages cost-effective real estate and efficient digital interactivity. It is a product of our new economy. We are creating a new store that lives squarely between the physical and digital storefronts.

Google: The Battle for George's Wallet

G WALLET • THE BATTLE FOR BIG DATA • THE CLOUD IS WHERE IT'S AT!

Many readers may recall the scene in *Seinfeld* when Jerry berates George about his oversized wallet:

> **Jerry:** Your back hurts because of your wallet. It's huge.
>
> **George:** This isn't just my wallet. It's an organizer, a memory, and an old friend.
>
> **Jerry:** Well, your friend is morbidly obese.

When Google attempted to explain to the public the concept of a mobile wallet, it turned to George. It produced a commercial that has Mr. Costanza's wallet exploding on the streets of New York with the tag line "Goodbye, wallet. The phone will take it from here" (www.youtube.com/watch?v=oy8QrYpSb88).

Everywhere you look in the press there are debates on the impeding mobile wallet. Free George of his back pain. Free George of his exploding cowhide wallet. Free George of his filing cabinet

Preaching "George" on the streets of New York

packed with coupons from Florida-area Exxon stations, miscella-
neous foreign currency, and receipts.

But does George want to be liberated? There is no question
that digital convergence has eliminated much of our wardrobe and
1990s gadget collection. Starting with our wristwatch, it has moved
to our instant camera and photo album, calculator, Rolodex, pocket
diary, eyewear, dog-eared maps, Game Boy, cosmetics bag, and
ATM cards.

Apple's app strategy has empowered garage-based developers
worldwide to create a virtual version of nearly all thingamabobs
known to the consumer. Apple's developer tool kit has managed to
increase its dominant position as the aspirational handheld. Apple
created this app economy to sell its products. It has managed to
continually outgun its competitors in the sheer number of miscel-
laneous applications created for its phones.

Some of these apps do emulate various compartments of a cowhide wallet: coupon-clipping apps, banking apps, money transfer apps, affinity deal of the day apps, gift card apps, Starbucks stored value apps, and so on.

But unlike George's wallet, the functionality of the digital wallet is neatly stored in phone folders, one click away from the cloud.

The solutions are exciting and feature-rich, but studies show that consumers are prepared to use only five to ten mobile apps, many of which are game or noncommerce utility apps. The reality (Costanza would protest, and I would hazard a guess that even Jerry Seinfeld would back him up) is that the existing wallet performs many of these tasks perfectly well and in many cases is closer than a click away.

G Wallet

Enter PayPal, Google Wallet, Isis (the AT&T, T-Mobile, and Verizon NFC payment consortium), and a proliferation of wallet businesses vying for George's attention. Now the pitch is more focused: one wallet that can tap on the cash register using contactless NFC technology to pay for goods and services, redeem store loyalty points, and accumulate coupons and other currency, all on your phone. The phone wallet can securely hold your credentials, enabling Visa, MasterCard, and Discover to enable transactions as if your plastic card were present. It also enables your medical insurance card, Social Security number, and driver's license to live behind the NFC tap. It enables tap-to-enter at the metro, tap-to-open-your-front-door, and tap-to-unlock-secure-data.

That is the pitch.

Tap-to-buy at the cash register seems one of the most exciting services. Google and Isis commercials show tap shoppers happily tapping all about town. Citibank has a billboard of the bride (of the future) proudly announcing that she bought her wedding dress with a tap of her Google Wallet–enabled phone.

The reality is that Tom's Diner, where George and Jerry debated the future of the wallet, will not have a NFC wallet reader for a long time. Only a minuscule sliver of the U.S. point of sale is open for contactless payment. VeriFone and other stakeholders in the value chain are working hard to provide the hardware to enable shoppers to tap and go, but we are years away from it actually happening.

George already has several wallets, and each wallet services a specific need:

- He has a PayPal account.
- He has stored his billing credentials in iTunes and Amazon.com.
- He can charge items to his phone bill.
- He has credit on his Starbucks card.
- His airline of choice has saved his credit card.

Google Wallet: brides on the run

All of the above wallets have a role and are used by consumers based on convenience or context or because they provide some economic benefit or reward.

The Google proximity wallet, which promises tap-and-buy convenience, also has a role. It is ideal for quick microtransactions: transit, convenience stores, fast-food restaurants. It will possibly not replace any of George's existing wallets; it will add a new one.

When George needs to run out on an errand or to the gym, he can leave his physical wallet at home, knowing that this mobile surrogate will pay for the taxi and a mineral water. Like a $20 bill in the pouch of our shoe or the pocket of our sweatpants, the phone will store this mobile cash.

We are not likely to have one universal wallet. We use different wallets for different purchases. We will naturally reach for one wallet for large-ticket purchases such as wedding dresses, another for a candy bar at the corner store, and a separate wallet to buy virtual credits on Facebook.

The Battle for Big Data

Though we think everyone is vying for the wallet, the real battle is for the "Big Data" that can be extracted from a payment relationship with the consumer. In a world where Google makes $7 in advertising revenue on every smartphone and tablet sold in North America (iOS and Android alike) (www.factbrowser.com/facts/4307/), the wallet creditable could drive this up by a multiple of ten.

Apple, Google, and the disenfranchised wireless carriers want to be that wallet. That is where many companies will make their fortunes over the next decade. In a world in which media companies are demanding more context and attention to their digital advertising spend, the impulse micropayment wallet is the new media mecca.

Which mobile wallet will win? Study after study shows that the driver of m-commerce adoption is *convenience* and the inhibitor of m-commerce is the degree of trust (of lack thereof). The winning wallet will be the one that is closest to the mobile consumer's point of decision. The winning wallet will enable an impulse purchase with minimal interruption and great fluidity. Finally, the winning wallet will likely debit and credit from trusted brands whose logos are laminated on retail doors across the United States.

Large retailers are likely to fight back with their own loyalty wallets. Those retailers' agendas are different from those of Isis and Google. They are focused on reducing their margin. A large part of their margin goes to third-party financial service companies. Walmart grudgingly pays the transaction toll (interchange) to the card companies if a shopper uses a card or card emulator. For Walmart, cash is cheap(er).

We use a lot of cash in the United States, and retailers such as Walmart would like to keep it that way. Some people may be surprised to find out that approximately 8 percent of U.S. households do not have bank accounts, which adds up to 17 million people. In addition to the nonbanking households, approximately 18 percent of U.S. households are underbanked (rely on pawnbrokers or loan sharks), which is a further 43 million people. Finally, there are cultural factors in many communities that make cash more attractive than a banking relationship.

There is an opportunity for Walmart and others to provide a viable mobile cash wallet to service the needs of those 60 million—plus consumers.

The Cloud Is Where It's At!

Tap-to-buy proximity wallets using Near Field Communication (NFC) technology are superbly elegant but are in early trials and do not have the ubiquity to be seamless and shopper-friendly. The main problem with those wallets is their developers, the banks. Banks tend to focus on legacy touch points such as point of sale, which have many moving parts and stakeholders. Banks want to continue doing business as usual.

A service outside this mold that has succeeded is Barclays' Pingit, which behaves more like an SMS than a banking application. There's no new wallet here; Pingit simply ties your banking (ATM) card to your phone number to enable you to use the number to transfer cash in the same way you communicate with friends. It also has a viral element: peer-to-peer instant transfer makes the wallet self-propagating and is the reason for the runaway success of the service.

We need to be mobile natives: think instant; think viral. For the U.S. retailer, the phone Internet may the closest to the checkout of choice for shoppers. While shoppers wait for a store to read their phones at the cash register, the final factor that will win them is always-on, always-ready checkout in a secure digital cloud.

Which cloud checkout will win?

- Amazon.com will win because its Kindle Fire "wallet" is bundled with a store. It has a convenient form factor with a frictionless checkout in the digital cloud wherever and whenever you need it.

- Google will win if it moves its wallet focus away from bricks and mortar and focuses on its strengths across all screens in the cloud.

- Visa's V.me and MasterCard's PayPass service, which have the trust of consumers, will win if they can create a quick checkout, eliminating the clumsy data entry that leads to abandoned shopping carts on the small screen.

- PayPal and Square mobile payment will win if their owners, eBay and Starbucks (respectively), can muscle them into mainstream bricks-and-mortar. Consumers demand ubiquity before they are prepared to adopt.

- And then there is Apple, which (of course) will win because it already has a cloud wallet for digital goods called iTunes. It will be dominant if it can expand its Apple Store EasyPay wallet trial to a physical goods "iShop" service using NFC commerce tags to turn any media into a shop-and-ship experience.

The winner will be the solution that does not try to be a universal wallet but is a *specific* checkout of choice for a *targeted* lifestyle or demographic. The winner will be the solution that can emulate the impulse nature of the mobile consumer. As Starbucks advocates: Pay faster; sip slower.

Mr. Costanza, what do you think?

Hot Topic:
Sell, Sell, Sell!

USING BARNEY'S PLAYBOOK • "PIN IT" •
ACTIVATION, ACTIVATION, ACTIVATION •
AND THEN CONVERSION

There are many valuable lessons to be learned from sitcoms. In *How I Met Your Mother*, Barnabus "Barney" Stinson's whatever-works seduction playbook has become barroom lore. Barney's goal is to close the sale, and each pickup strategy requires a fair about of creative marketing.

Granted, we may not all use Barney's "Lorenzo von Matterhorn" move. (Using a fake website, smartphone, and exotic name would not be a good tactic for every brand.) However, there is no question that mobile commerce demands a pickup playbook.

There is only a small window of engagement on a mobile phone. Selling requires quick one-liners. How can you make a value statement within a few seconds of attention? How can you connect with your consumer on a fast-moving mobile screen? And how can you move the would-be buyer from "I intend to buy" to "I will buy"?

Using Barney's Playbook

Farhan Ahmad, the director of emerging payments at Discover Financial Services, the issuer of the Discover Card, the third largest credit card brand in the United States, explains that "Mobile payment is a small subset of mobile commerce. Mobile commerce is primarily about shopper engagement and marketing." To paraphrase Farhan: *We need to develop a pickup strategy before we can close the sale.*

What mobile marketing mechanisms will engage with mobile shoppers and stay connected and relevant all the way to the cash register? Twitter's microblogging, Facebook's community building, foursquare's crowd sourcing, and Google Offers are all valuable tools, but any brand or retailer that is committed to a digital strategy across all its customers' screens needs to establish a *direct* relationship with shoppers.

One would think that Facebook, for example, as crowd sourcing central for the Web, would have the ability to compete with Amazon.com and PayPal. Facebook's director of business development, David Fisch, calls it the natural shopping mall.

Though Fisch is correct that "social" and "commerce" are natural allies, Facebook has not delivered on its promise to leverage its millions of customers to shop cross-channel. Pundits in 2012 predicted that sales of physical goods through Facebook and other social networks would jump from $5 billion to $30 billion by 2015. But Facebook folk are there to meet, not to shop.

Banana Republic and Old Navy tried to monetize their Facebook community by opening stores inside the social network. After underwhelming results they shut their virtual doors. Other retailers, including Nordstrom and JCPenney, that tried to cash in on community have failed. Even GameStop, with its more than 4 million Facebook fans (who one may suppose are committed gamers and ideal impulse shoppers) shut up shop after six months.

"Pin It"

A key strategy for a brand or retailer is to start a relationship in the social Web but as soon as possible to develop a *direct* loyal relationship with the consumer. A loyalist loves your product, and love begets "love to own."

The only two-way targeted channel to move the shopper across the retail touch points is via the shopper's mobile phone number. Why? Because once a direct, permission-based relationship is established between a shopper and a retailer, it cannot be disintermediated. Facebook, foursquare, Google, or Apple cannot get between you and your shopper.

Once there is a *direct* relationship, the brand can begin to develop a targeted and personalized communication channel. This will improve brand recall and conversion rates. Look at Estée Lauder's messaging experience across its brands. The more multimedia and the more targeted shopping options, the higher click-through rates (CTRs) and conversion:

- *Text message* with a link to product *information* generates 1x conversion (CTR).
- *Text message* with a link to product *shopping* generates 3x conversion (CTR).
- *Multimedia message* with a link to product *shopping* generates 6x conversion (CTR).

A message to an opt-in shopper (a brand loyalist) with a clear shopping call to action drives conversion results.

For that reason Pinterest will outperform Facebook on commerce activity. Clicking a Facebook "Like" button is a social affirmation; however, clicking a Pinterest "Pin It" button sends an I-want-it-and-you-should-too message.

Like other direct-to-consumer (D2C) channels, mobile messaging should deliver concrete results. A good mobile marketing service provider will be able to show the brand a projected return-on-investment (ROI) calculator. The key to building a loyalty channel strategy is to articulate how you intend to effectively *opt-in* the shopper and what your key performance indicators are, including which retail touch points you need the loyalty channel to connect to in order to drive your sales.

Activation, Activation, Activation

It is all about activation. When Amazon.com designed its Price Check app, it offered comparison shoppers several activation channels: MMS, SMS, voice, scan, and manual form input. Activation needs to be on the shopper's terms.

Activation triggers include 2D codes (QR), tapping NFC tags, and direct-from-mobile-phone text opt-ins. Opt-in channels include an app download or directly off a website, product and on-shelf call-to-action.

Here are some ways that retailers and brands can adopt an activation strategy with their store or product.

1. Click

The Web is probably the most logical place to start for most brands, as it extends their existing consumer relationship management (CRM) opt-in and offers shoppers a choice of channel. As in all marketing, shoppers should be given a choice of channels. Enabling opt-ins through Web forms facilitates the change from large-screen to small-screen messaging that is closer to the point of purchase and point of decision.

The key is to immediately engage on the mobile channel after the Submit button is pressed. (For a good example of this, go to www.maccosmetics.com and view the sign-up page.)

2. Scan

2D codes are everywhere on paper media, and they're cheap and easy to implement. Scan and move the shopper to the Web. However, the long-term goal is to move shoppers to a two-way opt-in relationship, so speak to your technology vender about how to do this. If you want to move directly to the mobile Web, make sure you enable messaging opt-in on the landing page. Without this possibility, this is an anonymous click. The brand does not know who the shopper is and has no opportunity to reengage with this potential customer.

An alternative activation channel is image recognition technology, which enables consumers to take a photo of a product or advertisement and send it to a cloud-based service that recognizes the image and sends back an offer or communication. Augmented reality (AR) is an extension of this technology, enabling more virtual interactivity and animation around the image recognition technology.

One substantial marketing hurdle to scan or photo activation is that it requires a bespoke application and is not standard or native to a phone. If a brand or retailer is required to spend marketing dollars to drive an application download, does it pervert your goal of driving your product and service?

3. Tap

Near Field Communication (NFC) is native to newer phones in the market; it seems to be all about payments, but it is really more about proximity marketing. Tag a product or poster, and enable Tap2Opt-in, Tap2Web, Tap2Coupon, Tap2Shop. Think of tap as a more frictionless scan. Tap is contactless marketing that does not

CeeLo, tap high!

require an app and is native to a handset—always on and always a
tap away from activation. The challenge is building a critical mass
in the marketplace. Look to late 2012 and into 2013 for some reach
and frequency in your shopper base. Samsung's NFC TecTiles,
which allow consumers to program stickers with phone commands,
are the first step to what I refer to as "CommerceTiles", which will
enable tap-to-buy activation via any media.

4. Text

Text messaging is the only two-way channel that has widespread
adoption. Seventy-four percent of smartphone users use SMS, as
opposed to email at 14 percent. Text messaging is native to a phone
and enables brands and retailers to deliver a "rich content" relationship with shoppers that can drive brand loyalty and measurable sales. However, the two direct channels work well together.
Text complements email by providing an actionable reminder that
reinforces the email blast. Focus on driving text-based opt-in to a

monthly or weekly subscription with brand loyalists, and use text messaging to mobilize existing promotions and engagements that lead to purchase.

In-app alerts are often viewed as being similar to SMSs as they emulate the SMS function on a phone. The only caution about this messaging channel is that it is tied to a bespoke application on an iOS, Android, or Windows phone. The relationship behind the alert is disintermediated by the Apple or Google. If the phone owner deletes the application then you have lost this relationship with the consumer. That is why, in July 2010, Google's YouTube jettisoned its Apple-bound phone application (and nascent community) and moved into the phone's mobile browser.

Apple's Passbook is an interesting hybrid. It has aggregated coupons, tickets, and vouchers into a super app. It allows brands to send a message to the phone with a ZIP file (digitally signed and blessed by Apple) that inserts a dynamic coupon, ticket or voucher into the Passbook. While the relationship is not two-way the content can be updated seamlessly by the brand and drives commerce activity.

Twitter is a very effective communication tool but again can confuse the messaging strategy. Text is an activation channel for your targeted, always-open customers. Twitter is a microblogging channel to a generalist community. Text = *circle* of trust; Twitter = informational *oblong*.

5. Dashboard

Perhaps the best strategy is to create an activation "dashboard" that enables shoppers to enter into a relationship on their terms. NFC, QR, and text can be combined into a single call to action. All activation channels can be serialized and tracked back to the media location to enable the brand to affiliate identify the store, media, and location.

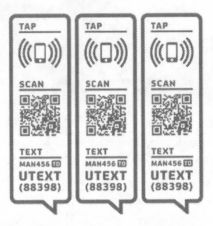

(Serialized) activation dashboard off any media

And Then Conversion

Once a brand or retailer has acquired a shopper's opt-in, it can pro-file the shopper based on geography or call to action. It can run minisurveys to better hone the relationship. Then it can provide SMS offers and deals with embedded trackable URLs. These deals

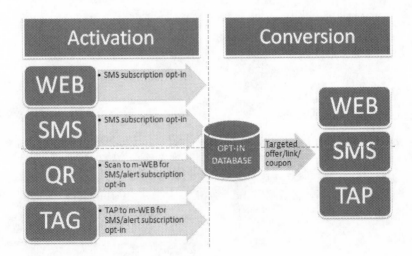

can be multiple-use or single-use, depending on the bricks-and-mortar point of sale (POS) or online redemption mechanism. As contactless wallets reach critical mass in the near future, tap coupons will also be a viable, more seamless option.

However, simple activation and simple conversion strategies continue to perform well. SMS coupons, for example, are showing up to 10 times conversion rates over email coupons in A/B tests. Offers sent to shoppers' mobile devices are consistently three times as likely to be redeemed as the same offers sent to a shopper's email address.

By creating a frictionless small-screen experience for the shopper, national retailers such as Hot Topic have repeatedly demonstrated measurable store-based and cloud-based checkout. In 2011, Hot Topic managed to generate nearly ten times the incremental sales off its loyalty community by leveraging the mobile channel.

Hot Topic believes that adding mobile messaging (SMS) to existing CRM/email marketing programs can produce a significant return on its marketing investment, especially during its holiday marketing efforts. Hot Topic had found that mobile messaging, deployed in addition to email, increases overall purchase intent and activity. We see the same strategy deployed by My Starbucks Rewards by using a clear SMS activation channel on its push advertising.

As technology changes, the principles of loyalty marketing remain the same.

Facebook, Privacy, and Big Data

THE DIGITAL COMMONS • WHAT WOULD AL
FRANKEN DO? • TRANSPARENCY, PLEASE!

We all are aware that social check-ins and social graph information are somehow connected to our ability to target and drive sales. If trust helps us build the relationship with new-age consumers, the desire for privacy is the unraveler.

We have private and a public shopping faces. We know that the digital world's business models run on "Big Data." Big Data is all about assembling enough digital history to intelligently interpret and predict behavior and trends to increase shopping relevance and ultimately sales.

We do not want to know that Big Data is linked to Big Brother; however, somewhere there is a social line on which the public and private collide.

In April 2012, a Moscow-based mobile developer launched a social application called Girls Around Me. This is an app that uses publicly available data from Facebook and foursquare's application programming interfaces (APIs) data that are completely permission-based. The Girls Around Me app (understandably) riled the press. The Cult of Mac blog's headline read "This Creepy App Isn't Just Stalking Women Without Their Knowledge, It's A Wake-Up Call About Facebook Privacy." CNET's op-ed was titled "Girls Around Me and the End of Internet Innocence."

The Digital Commons

However, the Girls Around Me application is simply another in a long list of controversial services that use information that is floating about the digital commons. The Russian company i-Free, which developed the app, could not understand the kerfuffle, claiming that it has been used as a scapegoat foursquare for the privacy debates whirling about Washington, D.C. Honestly, it has every right to be confused.

Retailers are at the center of the privacy debate. A few years ago consumers followed brands. Now brands follow channel-indifferent consumers. If stores are only one retail touch point to engage consumers, consumers' location and other sociodemographic data become essential. However, we do not know how to navigate this new opportunity, and we are alienating the very consumers we are trying to serve.

Walgreens called mobile check-in the new local flyer. It enables targeted information to be sent to willing, actively engaged shoppers. However, how can location be used to find shoppers when they are not actively checking in using applications such as foursquare? The negative media response to a service crossing the data collection line is a flag to anyone navigating these murky waters.

Where is the line? Clearly the industry is confused and responding to privacy in reactive knee jerks instead of thoughtful best practices. The problem is the complexity and sensitivity of social data. Combining location check-in with a social profile is a potent privacy cocktail. Brands and retailers trying to connect to shopper can be caught in the same maelstrom.

Every time the privacy issue hits the press, we act surprised. Remember the Dutch website Please Rob Me? A check-in at a bar means you are at the bar. It also means you are *not* at home. Immediately, we raise our our eyebrows. But that is publicly available information.

After headlining articles in Mashable through to Slashdot, the site rebranded itself as a benevolent attempt at "Raising awareness about over-sharing." The site now explains that:

> Services like Foursquare allow you to fulfill some primeval urge to colonize the planet. A part of that is letting everyone know you own that specific spot. . . . The danger is publicly telling people where you are. This is because it leaves one place you're definitely not . . . home.

In spite of these concerns, location applications continue to be apps du jour. At SXSW, the annual music and interactive festival in Texas, the Highlight app was downloaded by every Austin groupie to actively find connections in the crowds. Highlight required that users share their Facebook social graph and expose their phone's location. Highlight used the data to connect them to other people with shared interests; however, if they did not manually turn off the application, it continued to share and share long after they returned home from Austin.

Most mobile data are collected by simple Facebook or Twitter logins and cookieing of our browser and in-app activity. The data are used to improve profile and target advertising. Because of this, Big Data is the new gold rush for companies such as Facebook, Apple, and Google. The winner will gain access to all of the Big

Data that surrounds the consumer wallet activity. It is like a global Human Genome Project: a deluge of information. As shopkeepers we need to better understand how to use shopping "DNA" to help inform retail behavior and not spook our customers.

What Would Al Franken Do?

What should Al Franken (the chairman of the Senate Subcommittee on Privacy, Technology and the Law) and the nice folks at the FTC be doing to help proactively in the face of the privacy headlines? Should we tackle the issue by forcing companies such as Apple to reject apps that need to access the consumer's Unique Device Identifier (UDID), or are there simpler ways of addressing privacy issues?

As I discussed in my book *The Impulse Economy*, mobile misdemeanors get more press. The phone is hyperpersonal and therefore under more scrutiny. A mobile phone houses family photos, your girlfriend's SMSs, business notes, and now even a commerce wallet. Location and social graph information can be a boon to your nightlife but can flip dramatically to Orwellian Big Brotherhood.

What we need is a simple way of explaining privacy to consumers. Do you present pages of legalese on the small screen or do you simply present a coy "accept" button? Are there icons and concise explanations that allow the consumer to better understand what information is shared and why.

Transparency, Please!

Retailers and brands need to work together to offer consumers tools that enable transparency.

A survey done by TRUSTe is telling. Thirty-eight percent of respondents identified privacy as their number one concern when using mobile applications. But, more important, 98 percent of respondents want more transparency and choice about the personal information mobile apps collect and share, especially as it relates to targeted advertising and geo-location data.

The Cult of Mac blog calls Girls Around Me a "wake-up call about privacy," but we seem to wake up and fall back asleep in quick succession.

Key mobile dating rules for retailers:

- Prove that you are who you are and not a digital charlatan.
- Encrypt your data and tell your customers that you have done so.
- Have a privacy statement that can be understood without the help of legal counsel.
- Give your customers as much choice as possible. If they control the pain, they can bear the pain.

Sleeping with the CMO

MEETING IN THE AISLE • TAG, YOU'RE IT! •
A FARAWAY VOICE

For thousands of years we have bartered and sold goods and services. Over the past hundred years we have refined a retail business model and strapped on solutions to adapt to new media and technology. However, mobile adoption has arrived with unnatural speed. It is inevitable that there will be some resulting discord in the way we spend budget and the way we adapt to legacy technology.

Retail is not wounded or dying; it is vibrant and evolving. We may sell in new places via new channels, but we will inevitably move to more effective models of commerce. There is an invisible hand, and it is clutching a mobile phone.

According to various research data provided by Flurry, comScore, and Alexa, retailers and brands spend 29 percent of their budget on print even though the time consumers spend on print has dwindled to 6 percent of their day. We spend only 1 percent of our budget on mobile media, although it occupies 23 percent of our customers' attention.

This chart underscores how we silo budgets and is indicative of the old economy, where the store was at the center of consumers'

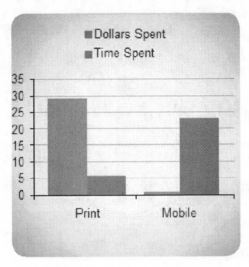

Flip mobile spending on its head

world. However, if we flip mobile on its head, it neatly offsets print deficits. Ad spend and time spend harmonize.

The mobile channel aids and complements other media channels. We now live in a cross-screen economy, and we need to stop buying media on isolated screens and in isolated media. Consumers' path to purchase now zigzags across various concurrent media channels and does not often end at the traditional cash register. Innovations and business models are no longer pegs on a linear washing line but are more analogous to three-dimensional putty.

There is one common thread, however: brands are putting money into channels that directly connect them with targeted consumers.

Meeting in the Aisle

I discussed this with Gene Keenan, who is the vice president of mobile solutions for Isobar, a leading digital communications agency.

Before Gene was a mobile aficionado he was the chef for the rock 'n' roll band the Grateful Dead for twelve years. What do rock 'n' roll, cooking, and mobile communications have in common? "There are lots of chefs in the retail kitchen," says Gene. "Media is divided. One campus handles POS, another campus marketing. But mobile has forced us to reconsider the way we work internally and the way we interact with our consumers and, most important, how we allow our consumers to interact with us."

Things get even more complex. It takes a considerable amount of effort to get departments to talk to one another. At the same time, the technology solutions that we implement horizontally across the company may need time to be incubated and will reach critical adoption only over a course of years. It is hard to work together when the technology underpinning your customer service, your marketing, and your profit goals is in perpetual flux. Here is a good illustration of the problem.

Many readers are aware of the 1987 Apple video that described a so-called knowledge navigator, a personal assistant that would help you keep appointments, find content share documents, etc. When you watch the YouTube clip at www.youtube.com/watch?v=HGYFEI6uLy0, is your reaction:

1. "Wow, 1987, how prophetic is Apple?"

or

2. "Wow, twenty-two years is a long time to launch Siri!"

Apple knew that to create a voice recognition system that would be seamless and adopted by its consumers might take a number of years. The futuristic video, made in 1987, is set in 2011 (prescient).

Apple is a technology company. It has interdepartmental staying power. However, how can a retailer or a brand bridge the gap between developing a technology solution that services its marketing vision and one that serves its customers' immediate needs? In a world where mobile makes for strange bedfellows, much of the innovation and business common sense required to navigate the disruption in the retail space is dependent on getting the key stakeholders in your store to work together.

The chief information officer (CIO) and chief marketing officer (CMO) need to meet in the aisle as technology and consumer adoption evolve. Normally the CIO follows the product and tries to increase efficiency, while the CMO follows the peripatetic consumer and tries to be relevant. The two do not hang out much. That has to change.

Tag, You're It!

CIOs strive to collect operational data, such as product description, price, origin, shelf life, and storage location. CIOs rightly believe that this will increase their insight into the supply chain, tracking everything from jeans to jelly. Walmart's CIO has mandated electronic "smart" tags (EPCs) on all of the retailer's vendors' products. The EPCs will enable it to automate the movement of products from the pallets in the distribution center to store shelves to shoppers' baskets. The tags will enable smart replenishment decisions, giving individual stores insight into their inventories and sales. All exciting stuff for CIOs.

With a smarter phone in your customers' hands, the CIO can work with store operations to enable shoppers to better interact with some of these data, making their shopping experience more effective and at the same time helping the CMO drive the all-important engagement with customers.

There is a cost to all this; however, in a world in which retailers need to count clicks to commerce, using existing merchandising solutions combined with shoppers' needs, this effort can pay dividends.

Finally the shopper and the shopkeeper may be approaching parity. In September 2012, Wal-Mart Stores Inc. began testing a Scan & Go system allowing shoppers to scan items using their phones and then pay at a self-checkout counter. A fast shopper is making for a fastest, more cost effective store.

Solutions like these will ultimately provide simpler shopper engagement and accelerate the path to purchase. Tethering the shopping experience to the shopper's phone will help the industry build a closer relationship with the shopper, hopefully building trust and closing more deals.

A Faraway Voice

Some pundits talk about the death of the phone and the rise of pervasive computing. They talk about a world in which every touch point will be a connected device. It is true that the term "online" has lost its meaning and perhaps with its demise, the term "mobile" may also lose its meaning. In a world where everything is now mobile or portable, is the concept of a telephone an artifact of history along with typewriters and turntables? With Google Goggles and Nike FuelBands, shouldn't we not focus on data and how it is collected and disseminated? Is the phone's historic function subsumed into the world of connected utility?

This book is advocating for the return of the phone, the importance of the phone as the great communicator. The value of the phone remains the pictures and texts that connect the device to other devices. The value is in the social Venn diagram between you and others. The reason we keep our phone under the pillow and on the coffee table is that it connects us at all times to people and associations that are in our circle of trust.

Ironically, the problem we face as social, relationship-loving brands has become the phone. The problem is simply the power of a smarter phone. The Galaxy S III (and its daunting speed of 2,600 times as great as the Apollo Guidance Computer) confuses brands into believing that they are trying to connect to a computer and not a person. We need to bring back the love.

In the not-too-distant future, when all phones become smart, we will hopefully lose the "smart" appendage and return to the job of connecting to the *phone*. If the derivation of the word telephone is made up of *tēle*, "faraway," and *phōnē*, "voice," the mobile phone simply provides a social voice, a gaming voice, a retail voice; our goal as brands and retailers is connecting to that *faraway voice*. As brands and retailers move more budget into directly connecting with shoppers, we must hope and trust that the number scrawled on the barroom matchbox leads to a second date.

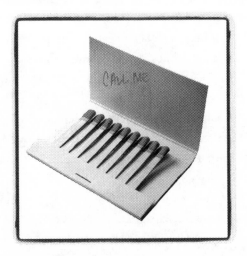

416-505-7410. Twitter @impulseeconomy. www.theimpulseeconomy.com. facebook.com/impulseeconomy. G+ impulseeconomy.

Printed in the United States
By Bookmasters